JUMPING OUT OF BED

Poems by Robert Bly

Woodcuts by Wang Hui-Ming

Jan. 29 , 199

雨
整天
不停

風
吃起
下去 2 小子

時了

Books on W.B.

Banyen

WHITE PINE PRESS

ISBN 0-934834-08-3

Originally published, in a slightly different version, by Barre Publishers.

Grateful acknowledgement is made to Slow Loris Press, the Oxhead Press, and to the editors of the following magazines in which these poems have earlier appeared: *Cafe Solo, Chelsea, Massachusetts Review, Field, Antioch Review, The Phoenix, Lillabulero, Panjandrum, The Record, Road Apple Review,*and *Stone Drum.* "After Long Busyness" first appeared in *Poetry* and "Like the New Moon" in the *Iowa Review.*

Photograph of Robert Bly by Elaine Maloney

This publication was made possible, in part, by a grant from the New York State Council on the Arts.

Published by White Pine Press
              76 Center Street
              Fredonia, New York 14063

JUMPING
OUT OF BED

All around me men are working;
but I am stubborn, and take no part.
The difference is this:
I prize the breasts of the Mother.
                    —*Tao Te Ching*

I came out of the Mother naked,
and I will be naked when I return.
The Mother gave, and the Mother takes away,
I love the Mother.
                    —*Old Testament, restored*

4.

A Sitting Poem
There is a solitude like black mud!
Sitting in the darkness singing
I can't tell if this joy
if from the body, or the soul, or a third place!

5.

Listening to Bach
There is someone inside this music
who is not well described by the names
of Jesus, or Jehovah, or the Lord of Hosts!

6.

When I woke, new snow had fallen.
I am alone, yet someone else is with me,
drinking coffee, looking out at the snow.

SIX WINTER PRIVACY POEMS

1.

About four, a few flakes.
I empty the teapot out in the snow,
    feeling shoots of joy in the new cold.
By nightfall, wind,
the curtains on the south sway softly.

2.

My shack has two rooms; I use one.
The lamplight falls on my chair and table,
and I fly into one of my own poems—
I can't tell you where—
as if I appeared where I am now,
in a wet field, snow falling.

3.

More of the fathers are dying each day.
It is time for the sons.
Bits of darkness are gathering around them.
The darkness appears as flakes of light.

LOOKING AT CLOUD BANKS
BELOW THE PLANE WINDOW

Hills of cloud, mountains of mist below.
What are they? Troll-heads,
tufts of forgetfulness,
childhood stories, dreams of someone's death.

Perhaps a burbling up of blind affection . . .
The clouds are affectionate creatures
with their backs turned to us,
crouched over a smiling landscape beneath.

How different these tuffy bodies are from ours!
They are secretive, but do not cling,
are not afraid of a storm,
willing to dissipate in the wind . . .

THE POEM

Coming nearer and nearer the resonating chamber
the poem begins to throw itself around
fiercely,
silent stretches of snow,
grass waving for hundreds of miles.

Intent pierces into hard wood, which grows dense
from inside, something mad penetrates
the wood,
something alive, something
human, like a violin that reverberates with thought.

A fierce intent that nature does not know of
drives inside the poem,
changes it,
thicken it with sober weight;
it is something dense, a human madness.

A DOING NOTHING POEM

After walking about all afternoon
barefoot, in my shack,
I have grown long and transparent . . .
like the sea slug
who has lived along doing nothing
for eighteen thousand years.

TONGUES WHIRLING

You open your mouth, I put my tongue in,
and this wild universe-thing begins!

Our tongues together are two seagulls
    whirling high above the Great Lakes,
two jellyfish floating under a Norwegian moon!

Suddenly we are with the fallen leaves,
    blowing along the soaked roads.
My hand closes so firmly around you
and I feel the sea rising
    and falling
as we go ashore . . .

We are two turtles with wings!

We are rolling together, head down,
through oceans of mother air!

We are two tumbleweeds hurrying through the universe.

WALKING IN DITCH GRASS

The spring wind blows dissatisfactions
and mad architects, two-mile long tails—

and my shoes like whales
eat the grass; they sweep through
the grass, eating
up the darkness.

The night is windy. Sleek cows fly
across the sky. Samson
is angry. It must be this grass we need
to balance our dissatisfactions,
this grass, blowing, open, and uneven.

ANOTHER DOING NOTHING POEM

There is a bird that flies through the water.
It is like a whale ten miles high!
Before it went into the ocean,
it was just a bit of dust from under my bed!

THE MAGNOLIA GROVE
For Michael Bullock

Wang Wei: The mountain receives the last sunshine of fall.
Flocks fly off following the first that leaves.
Occasionally something emerald flashes in the trees.
The evening dark has nowhere to settle down.

P'ei Ti: Settling down at dusk from the dome of light
bird voices get mingled with the river sounds.
The path beside the river winds off into the distance.
Joy of solitude, will you ever come to an end?

木風榮玉輝
悲歡飲餘明
知身還玉高侶
彩翠時分
明月荒
莫笑所

同祿紉衣邊
蒼蒼崖日時
鳥鳴乳
運孫屋
路孫深玄
興何时也

THE CREEK BY THE LUAN HOUSE

Wang Wei: Autumn rain and sudden winds.
              The water plunges, bouncing off the rocks.
              Waves leap aimlessly over each other.
              The white heron is alarmed and lands.

P'ei Ti: A man could hear the water-sound far off.
              I walk down looking for the ford.
              Ducks and egrets swim away, and then
              veer back, longing to be near people.

擘窠圭稜
騷秋風中
廢墟石臨海
緲沙年飛
幾白鷗
飛聲下

同泳 紀靈迪

散辭喧
抱庸涼步
向南岸況
兔鶴渡時
時飲近人

SLEEPING FACES

Tonight the first fall rain washes away my sly distance.
I have decided to blame no one for my life.
This water falls like a great privacy.
Letters sink into the desk,
the desk sinks away, leaving an intelligence
slowly learning to talk of its own suffering.
The muttering of thunder is a gift
that reverberates in the roof of the mouth.
Another gift is a child's face in a dark room
I see as I check the house during the storm.
My life is a blessing, a triumph, a car racing through the rain.

A NIGHT IN DECEMBER

On this windy December night two children lost their way.
"Birds ate the womb-shaped seeds we dropped in the moonlight."
("You know we left so early the moon was still out.")
"Come in, do not be frightened, children."

How odd that I feel a connection between the feminine
and this windy December night! Or is it the feminine?
When Paris took Helen away, he kept the moon in a pouch.
Inside the salmon's stomach, the cook finds the wedding ring.

"Come in, do not be frightened, children!"
Why do men need this fear? Some are torn in pieces,
other men lengthen out years on islands . . .
This night calls: men will die for this night.

SIX IMAGES FOR DEATH

Death throws a shadow on our shadow, as if it were a tree.
We then are pasture grass the cows eat unevenly.
We are a weight on a string swaying from the motion of the planet.
We are a rock tunnel through which chill air rushes.
Mammoths feel the air rise through their hollow legs.
The leaves above the grass pick up the wind and rustle.

AFTER LONG BUSYNESS

I start out for a walk at last after weeks at the desk.
Moon gone, plowing underfoot, no stars; not a trace of light!
Suppose a horse were galloping toward me in this open field?
Every day I did not spend in solitude was wasted.

CHRYSANTHEMUMS
(planted for Tao Yuan Ming, who likes them)

1.

Tonight I rode again in the moonlight!
I saddled late at night.
The horse picked his way down a dead-furrow,
guided by the deep shadows.

2.

A mile from the yard the horse rears,
glad. How magnificent to be doing nothing,
moving aimlessly through a nighttime field,
and the body alive, like a plant!

3.

Coming back up the pale driveway,
how calm the wash looked on the line!
And when I entered my study, beside the door,
white chrysanthemums in the moonlight!

FOR R·B· AND
WHO LOVE
MING'S
AND HIS
THEMUMS·

ALL THOSE
TAO YUAN
POETRY
CHRYSAN
H·M·

THE HILL OF HUA-TZU

Wang Wei: The birds fly away into the air that never ends;
the magnificence of fall comes back to the mountain.
Whenever I walk up or down Hua-Tzu hill,
my whole body feels confusion and inner suffering.

P'ei Ti: The sun goes down; there is wind sound in the pines.
Walking home I notice dew on the grass.
The white clouds look up at me from the tracks of my
        shoes.
The blue from the mountain touches my clothes.

THE WALNUT TREE ORCHARD

(An answering poem in which Wang Wei writes the first poem, then his friend P'ei Ti writes a poem answering it.)

Wang Wei: In the old days the serious man was not an "important
                person."
            He thought making decisions was too complicated for
                him.
            He took whatever small job came along.
            Essentially he did nothing, like these walnut trees.

P'ei Ti: I soon found nothing was a great joy to me.
            Look, you see, here I am! Keeping my ancient promise.
            Let's spend today just strolling around these walnut trees.
            The two of us will nourish the ecstasies Chuang Tzu
                loved.

ON A MOONLIT ROAD IN THE NORTH WOODS

I sit on the forest road,
cross-legged.
I am an oyster
breathing on his own shore.

*

Cars seldom use this road.
I looked up and down,
     no car coming, none would,
perhaps for hours . . .

*

All day my thoughts ran on in small rivulets
near some bigger flood.
Several times water
     carried me away:
then I was a cedar twig,
     a fish scale . . .

*

And what does the oyster think
on this forest road?
He thinks of his earlier life,
of meeting her again.

SOME NOVEMBER PRIVACY POEMS

I am comforted
by a crack in dry ground
nearly smoothed over with winter dust.

* * *

How marvellous to look out and see
the boulders
that have been gloomy since the earth began
now with a faint dusting of snow.

* * *

Mist: no one on the other shore.
It may be the trees I see have consciousness
and this desire to weep comes from them.

* * *

Most birds have gone south.
Grass heels over in wind.
The feminine hooves of the horse
stand side by side as he eats.

LIKE THE NEW MOON
I WILL LIVE MY LIFE

When your privacy is beginning over,
how beautiful the things are that you did not notice before!
A few sweetclover plants
along the road to Bellingham,
culvert ends poking out of driveways,
wooden corncribs, slowly falling,
what no one loves, no one rushes towards or shouts about,
what lives like the new moon,
and the wind
blowing against the rumps of grazing cows.

Telephone wires stretched across water,
a drowning sailor standing at the foot of his mother's bed,
grandfathers and grandsons sitting together.

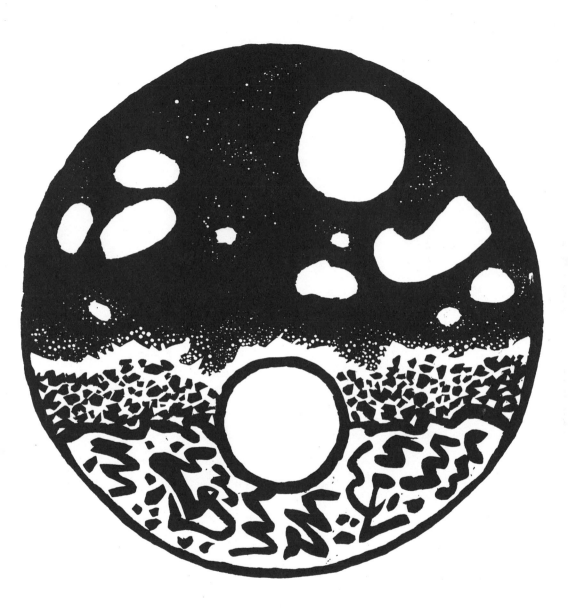

THINKING OF "THE AUTUMN FIELDS"

1.

Already autumn begins here in the mossy rocks.
The sheep bells moving from the wind are sad.
I have left my wife foolishly in a flat country,
I have set up my table looking over a valley.
There are fish in the lake but I will not fish;
I will sit silently at my table by the window.
From whatever appears on my plate,
I will give a little away to the birds and the grass.

2.

How easy to see the road the liferiver takes!
Hard to move one living thing from its own path.
The fish adores being in the deep water;
 the bird easily finds a tree to live in.
In the second half of life a man accepts poverty and illness;
praise and blame belong to the glory of the first half.
Although cold wind blows against my walking stick,
I will never get tired of the ferns on this mountain.

3.

Music and chanting help me overcome my faults;
the mountains and woods keep my body fiery.
I have two or three books only in my room.
The sun shining off the empty bookcase warms my back.
Going out I pick up the pine cones the wind has thrown away.
When night comes, I will open a honeycomb.
On the floor-throw covered with tiny red and blue flowers,
I bring my stocking feet close to the faint incense.

TURTLE CLIMBING FROM A ROCK

For Wang Hui-Ming

How shiny the turtle is, coming out
of the water, climbing the rock, as if
Buddha's body were to shine!
As if swift turtle wings swept out of darkness,
crossed some barriers,
and found new eyes.
An old man falters with his stick,
later, walkers find holes in black earth.
The snail climbs up the wet trunk glistening
like an angel-flight trailing long black banners.
No one finds the huge turtle eggs
lying inland on the floor of the old sea.